HOMEBUYER ROLLERCOASTER

HOMEBUYER
ROLLERCOASTER

THE BUYER'S GUIDE TO
SAVING YOUR MONEY & SANITY

MONICA BENITEZ

NEW YORK

LONDON • NASHVILLE • MELBOURNE • VANCOUVER

HOMEBUYER ROLLERCOASTER
THE BUYER'S GUIDE TO SAVING YOUR MONEY & SANITY

© 2020 **MONICA BENITEZ**

Published in New York, New York, by Morgan James Publishing in partnership with Difference Press. Morgan James is a trademark of Morgan James, LLC.
www.MorganJamesPublishing.com

ISBN 978-1-64279-509-7 paperback
ISBN 978-1-64279-510-3 eBook
ISBN 978-1-64279-541-7 Audio
Library of Congress Control Number: 2019935177

Morgan James is a proud partner of Habitat for Humanity Peninsula and Greater Williamsburg. Partners in building since 2006.

Get involved today! Visit
www.MorganJamesBuilds.com

For Dante and Dominic,
True love never ends
My reason
My motivation
The lights of my life
This book and everything I aspire to be
is in dedication to both of you.
I love you to never ends,
Mim

TABLE OF CONTENTS

	Introduction	*ix*
Chapter One	Buyers' Perspective—Where do I Start?	1
Chapter Two	Everything Happens for a Reason	7
Chapter Three	Home Sweet Home	15
Chapter Four	Homebuyer Blueprint	23
Chapter Five	Initial Requirements of Buying a Home	113
Chapter Six	Other People's Money	118
Chapter Seven	What's "The" Big Deal?	123
Chapter Eight	What's Next?	128
Chapter Nine	The Mental Game	134
	Conclusion	144
	This Is It!	144
	Acknowledgements	*153*
	Thank You!	*157*
	About the Author	*159*

INTRODUCTION

Are you ready to feel that sense of empowerment and joy that homeownership brings? Are you ready to take control of your stability and security? This is your moment to celebrate that you are ready to buy your home. Picking up this book means you are open and ready to see your dream of owning your home manifest into reality. Today is life-changing. Today you begin to take the journey to finally make owning your own home a part of your life's blueprint. Together we can make sure you're making moves in the direction that lead you to gaining the upper hand when buying your home, enhance who you already are, save yourself money and keep your sanity.

Get ready for the ride of your life that is so worth every moment! Over and over again I meet buyers that never thought being a homeowner would happen. They trust in the process and this is when the magic happens. This is when they begin to manifest their desires. In the end, they are so grateful to have been pushed when they needed the push, motivation, support, and that I never lose hope even when they lost hope in themselves.

As a tenant you never feel fulfilled until you receive an opportunity to own. In life there are no coincidences. There's a reason why you chose this book. The time is now to end the cycle of renting and begin the journey of homebuying. This book not only acts as a guide to the process of homeownership, but helps buyers understand that the homebuying process is a state of mind as you learn to dominate the ins and outs of buying a home. There are many homebuyer guides out there for you to choose from, but none that incorporate the element of your will to make it happen, your intention, your commitment to the transaction, and the commitment on behalf of your agent.

As a buyer's agent, I'm always looking for the best opportunities for my buyers. I help a buyer with many facets like prequalification, home selection, contracts, inspections, appraisal, etc. I negotiate and help a buyer navigate through the many steps in the buying process. There are many times that the buying process can get complicated and buyers can feel as if they are riding an emotional rollercoaster. I press forward and fight for their best interest and encourage them to trust in the process.

Many times I have been told, "You want this more than the buyer does!" or "You can't want it more than they do." I paid attention to my reaction the first time I was told this. At the time it made me feel that I needed to reflect. You might be saying to yourself, "She wants what?" I would lie if I told you these questions didn't get me thinking whether I want buyers to have their dream home more than they themselves did. I quickly realized that I do go above and beyond to make my buyers' dreams come true. I am selling the dream! My wish for them is to feel what every homeowner feels: a sense of empowerment, stability, and security. I am very passionate that everyone experiences this in their life, and I'm thankful for the opportunity to be a part of such a special milestone. It's why I feel as passionate about real estate as I do; and why I decided to create Homebuyer Rollercoaster: The Buyer's Guide to Saving Your Money & Sanity.

My motivation to write this book was my intuitive and unconditional love of selling. When my buyers become homeowners, they are so thankful for having been pushed forward. My focus is always solution-oriented, and I believe where there is a will there is a way. I educate my buyers to stop thinking like tenants and start thinking like investors, as every property you own is an investment in your growth and future. As I guided buyers through the process, I found that their biggest challenge wasn't credit, income, or down payment, but maintaining a positive mental state and controlling their emotions. They needed to stay focused and in a place of appreciation and gratitude so that they could attract a positive outcome and manifest their desires.

At times it can feel like an emotional rollercoaster as you learn to navigate the steps until you finally arrive at the closing table. Trusting in the process is key. When those keys are handed to you, my reward as your agent is seeing you experience that immense joy and sharing in that accomplishment of moving into your home.

Chapter One

BUYERS' PERSPECTIVE— WHERE DO I START?

Your story might have started a little like this:

"We are in the information age, so why is it that I don't know where to start? With information at an instant, why is it that I can't find my way? Friends that say one thing and articles that claim another. Workshops, workbooks, webinars … done them all. I've been doing a little house hunting for the perfect house in the perfect location on my own, of course. I don't need a realtor; I can do this on my own. How complicated can it be?

"Either way, I'm waiting to save more money, and thankfully I'll be getting my next pay raise soon. I'm working my way through school part-time and waiting for my current car lease to expire. Especially since it's at a high interest rate because I have a couple of collections on my credit. Interest rates keep rising, home prices continue to rise, but that's okay ... soon I will buy when home values make that dramatic drop that I'm sure is coming! Maybe then I'll buy a short sale and get that next great deal or better yet a foreclosure. By then I will have enough money saved. Someone told me I need to buy with twenty percent down, and I heard that webinar that said it's best to obtain a home loan and put at least twenty percent down to avoid paying mortgage insurance. I do not want to pay mortgage insurance!"

Six Years Later

"I'm twenty-six now and working full-time. Now I really feel ready to take that step into homeownership! I now have $35,000 in student loans and I desperately need a new car and if anyone knows how hard I have worked it's me! I deserve that brand-new car, and this time I will qualify for a better interest rate, so I can afford the car of my dreams. I'll just spread the payments into seventy-two months instead of paying $700 a month I can now get the car of my dreams for $590 and financed so it will be mine! By the time it's up, I'll be making even more money and I'll be able to buy my own home, and here's the kicker ... I'm improving my credit score!

"I finally met the man of my dreams in college, where we had endless hours of talking about our future goals. I'm so in love, and I can't wait to plan the wedding! How exciting! We have saved about $20,000 together, and I do have a new car that still has three more years left before it's all paid off. I finally finished school, and my full-time job is going well. This couldn't have come at a better time. Once we are settled in, we can start saving again! This time together to finally buy a home! I'm so tired of renting and paying someone else's mortgage. Every year the rent goes up, this place gets older, and the landlord pays less and less attention to this property and my needs. Everything will work itself out."

Four Years Later

"I'm thirty and I just got my master's degree, I'm married, got a new car, and things are just perfect. Within the next couple of years, we will have enough money to buy our home. By then, we will have saved our twenty percent down payment that I was told would be all I needed in order to buy. Besides, I've done all the seminars, webinars, and workshops for new homebuyers.... How much could have changed?

"Surprise! Life just keeps getting better and better; I'm pregnant and we are expecting our first child. What a blessing! Only thing is we are so crowded here in this one-bedroom apartment, and there's no yard. Our puppy is growing, and the baby is coming. We are a little shy of our twenty percent down payment and have been paying $1,800 in rent, $60,000 combined in student loans, $1,200 combined for car payments, and even though we are college graduates, we make about $80,000 in our combined household income. Oh, and a few credit cards that I'm still paying down from repairs around the house since the landlord never answers our emails. And I can't forget that the baby needs things, too."

Does any of this sound familiar? Did you ever plan out your life and realize things don't always work out as expected?

Have you ever seen yourself in any of these predicaments? Even though they are all things that bring you joy.... What could have been done differently to put you and your family in a stronger buying position?

Recognize the Value of an Asset vs a Liability

We work hard and we all like to be rewarded. However, a car is used to get from point A to point B. It's a depreciating asset. It will not make you money. On the contrary; it depreciates in value the minute you drive out of the dealership. Yes, you can use it as a tool to help establish credit, but if you do not plan wisely it can be one of the many things that keep you from qualifying for a home loan. This does not mean you can't have a car, but shift that payment into one that's more reasonable and allows you to grow your bank account. Once you own your first home, then you can decide if a high car payment is a wise choice.

Why Rent When You Can Buy?

There are many programs out there to help buyers purchase their home. I have sold homes with as little as a first, last, and one month's security deposit the total of which was $5,000. Closing cost fees and your mortgage payment equal the same amount as your rent payment. These programs are government funded, so they are not everlasting. Once the money runs out, the program no longer exists. However, there are always new programs rolled out, grants, etc. These are all available to make our dream of homeownership come true.

The key here? Don't wait. Act. When you pay rent, you are not only throwing away your money, you are also losing money. If you would have owned a home, you would have been earning the equity in that home's growth. In addition, as a homeowner you have so many benefits that as a tenant are not available to you. In the scenario above, the average rent that has been paid is upwards of $172,000, the equivalent of which could have been a substantial down payment. Many of us have never calculated how much money has been spent in rent during our lifetime. See the rental chart below. Where do you fall on this chart? We all need a roof over our heads, and I get that. However, it's not just the $172,000 that has been thrown away in rent; it's the equity that you could have made in the last five years of renting. In today's market, that represents about another $100,000 in addition to the tax benefits for homeowners. When we file our personal tax returns, we can deduct the interest paid throughout the year. There are also some costs that you pay when closing on a home that can be deducted on your tax returns.

Lastly, depending where you buy, here in Florida you also receive what's called Homestead Exemption, which is an exemption on your property taxes. In Florida, establishing homestead offers significant protection from creditor claims, as well as substantial real estate tax benefits.

Seek the Advice of a Realtor/Buyer's Coach

Allow yourself to be guided. Do you know the difference between a successful person and unsuccessful person? The difference is the influence of a mentor/coach, and even they have a mentor/

coach of their own. By investing in a Buyer's Coach you would have implemented a long-term plan long before the student loans, car debts, and $172,000 in rent payments. You would have been able to buy your home. Good news is that it's never too late. Buyer's Coaches specialize in every type of scenario, so embrace your current situation and contact a Buyer's Coach to mentor you.

HOW MUCH HAVE YOU SPENT IN RENT?

MONTHY RENT	3 YEARS	10 YEARS	15 YEARS	30 YEARS
$1,000	$36,000	$120,000	$180,000	$360,000
$1,250	$45,000	$150,000	$225,000	$450,000
$1,500	$54,000	$180,000	$270,000	$540,000
$1,750	$63,000	$210,000	$315,000	$630,000
$2,000	$72,000	$240,000	$360,000	$720,000
$2,250	$81,000	$270,000	$405,000	$810,000
$2,750	$99,000	$330,000	$495,000	$990,000
$3,000	$108,000	$360,000	$540,000	$1,080,000

Chapter Two

EVERYTHING HAPPENS
FOR A REASON

In this chapter, I'd like to show you some of my experiences in my real estate career and share the stories of a few of my customers and their journey. Just as I have helped them make their dreams come true, each one of my buyers also left an impact on my life.

The Story of Jackie

Here I am walking through a neighborhood with buyers that had been renting for many years. They have already spent over $100,000 in rent. They finally understand that throwing away money on rent has to stop and are ready to make the shift into homeownership. We are looking at resale homes and as we walk out and onto the sidewalk we notice a new construction development across the way.

Coming from the resale luxury market, this opens up a new avenue of business and begins my journey in the new construction market.

Setting the wheels in motion for educating, coaching and offering numerous buyers and investors the benefits of buying new construction.

Low down payments and seller contribution towards closing costs are a few of the incentives available. The impossible now becomes possible for many prospective buyers.

You may be asking yourself, "How does this relate to me?" I developed a very prosperous real estate career helping people just like yourself, and through the many buyers I have met and helped buy homes I created a system that helps you better understand the journey you will embark on in the homebuying process. When I meet with you, within the first ten minutes I know what you need.

I created what I call an "MRI" of my prospective buyer. Like a scan which goes beyond the surface, the "MRI" is a series of questions that allow me to get to know you at a deeper level. Unlike the typical questions realtors ask, I go beyond the surface, beyond the credit score, income, and money. But what is it that drives you? What is really motivating you to become a homeowner? What do you feel are your biggest obstacles? I discuss the rollercoaster of emotions that this process will bring to set expectations so you can better understand how this will be the ride of your life.

Through these questions I get to know your story. I know what you need emotionally. I create a connection with you at a soul level. That connection is what drives me to go above and beyond for "my people." That willingness to be open and share your deepest fears, needs, hopes, and dreams is my drive and motivation to fight for you and your dream. Each buyer becomes a part of my life. They each teach me something new and leave an imprint on my life. It's what makes me a better realtor, and in return a better help to my buyers. It's what makes me a better person, mother to my twin boys, sister, daughter, friend, Buyer Coach, Realtor Coach and now author. It's these connections that I make throughout my life with each of my buyers that drives me to push forward for them and their dreams. These are the connections that nourish my intuitive, unconditional love of selling. It's these candid moments of laughter and tears my buyers share with me that have motivated me to write this book. With their consent, I'll share their stories and their experiences of the homebuying process for the purpose of making a difference in your life as you will one day go through the process yourself. Their names have been changed to maintain their privacy.

Michael and Miranda's Story

My cell phone rang, and the number was a familiar one. My instinct told me I needed to stop what I was doing and be present for this person, whom I had much appreciation for. As I interrupted my early morning workout, I heard the voice of a person who I had connected with, and I knew this moment was going to be pivotal in her life.

"Monica, I'm not doing this. I'm not moving forward. I'm not buying this property with Michael. I'm not closing! I would rather lose my deposit than move forward and make this commitment with him; he's not the person I wish to own a home with. I'm sorry. I know everything you have done for me and I'm very appreciative, but I'm done, this is just not my time," Miranda says.

I felt her pain. I really did. But I also felt and knew that she was making what would be the biggest mistake and regret of her life. If I didn't show up for her right then and if I allowed her to let her feelings get the best of her, she would lose this property. So, there it went; I was now my buyer's therapist.

"Miranda let's put this in perspective. First, Michael is very nervous, and he, too, is going through a lot right now. It's the first time you are both ever becoming homeowners, which is something you both have always dreamed of. Now that it's coming true, it's scary. He has showed up for you throughout this entire transaction both emotionally and financially. When you had your moments, he called me and asked me to please believe in you both and continue to help you guys make this happen. He's a good man. Secondly, you won't buy a home with this man but gave him a child? You are a strong woman, and you're are going to close on this home and love very minute of it. You will thank me later," I promised.

I did lose a workout, but if I did not do that, Miranda and Michael would have lost something bigger: their dream. I couldn't live with that. When I contacted Miranda to ask for her blessing to share her story, she was very grateful. She shared with me that she was decorating the house, and that her neighbor is her long-lost childhood friend and they have reconnected. Miranda wasn't just decorating her house; she was building a life of memories in her new home. This for me was confirmation that everything happens for a reason. Anyone can sell a house. I sell homes. I sell the dream.

Leo's Story

Whether it's your first home, investment home, or commercial property, I always have to have the buyer's best interest in mind. Leo had a growing, thriving business that he had built from the ground up all on his own. He was a self-made man who employed a handful of people whom he referred to as "family." The call came in, and Leo sounded a bit excited yet anxious. I immediately picked up that this was an important matter. I knew this man was about his "people" like I am about "my people," so we have a genuine connection. I understood that the business decisions he made affected the people he most cared about.

"Monica, I need to expand my business, and I am out searching for land in Central Florida. I need a satellite office that warehouses my trucks and can have a small office with a bathroom and a small living space for my employees as they wait for overnight industrial trucks to load, unload, and repair medical supplies in a climate-controlled facility. I'm not too sure if I will get this contract, but I do have to have the facility ready to be able to grow so I need to make a savvy investment fast," he said.

No pressure, right? Leo was scoping out the area for warehouses. Warehouses could run upwards of a million dollars for the size he wanted and needed. However, I heard something totally different when he called me. I heard a man who was willing to gamble on a contract that wasn't certain in order to secure growth, continue to maintain his loved ones, and ensure job security for his employees who were like family. I respected and admired how this man took care of his people, and since I make connections at a soul level, I knew what I needed to do.

Leo needed a property that could house industrial vehicles with easy access to the highway, with living quarters, and some type of facility where medical equipment could be stored and repaired within a climate-controlled area. It also needed to be a reasonable price since the contract was not secure. Quite the challenge! Here's where my experience and expertise needed to show up. And it did.

Leo purchased a $230,000 three-bedroom, two-bathroom home for his employees on a large lot off the highway. It had a private airstrip with a 40,000 square foot hangar that could be converted into a temperature-controlled area with a small office and bathroom. Now, Leo had made a minimal investment so that if the contract did not work out, he could rent the home and receive an income. Leo was a businessman; he knew I could have steered him into the million-dollar warehouse and made a larger commission. I chose to look at what was in his best interest, and when you look out for the best interest of others, prosperity will come. Leo's business is thriving, and I put in that intention for him to succeed. In turn, when I contacted Leo for his blessing to share his story his response was, "Anything to help you succeed, Monica." Everything happens for a reason.

Like Leo and Miranda, I have many stories, all of which continue to reassure me of who I am and the strong ethics that my parents instilled in me and that I maintain in my real estate career. I am known as a "closer" in the business, and, yes, I do have a great amount of ambition. I do make a living from real estate. So, it's not that money doesn't matter, because it does. Money allows you to protect your loved ones, money allows you security and financial freedom.

However, it takes one's own personal journey to get to a place where you're not looking at the transaction just to make your commission, but you make decisions based on the best interest of the buyer. Then, the money just comes, and my buyers will benefit. So, this is my story. Sometimes life carves a path for you that was not what you envisioned in your life plan. But you trust that there's a lesson to learn or an experience to grow from. After much thought, I decided to make a shift in my fifteen-year career in construction and development. First, I felt I needed freedom. I knew I was not living to my true potential, and thanks to my sister Lisa, my forever best friend, my backbone, and biggest fan helped me to my true self. She reassured me that what I wanted and needed was not just freedom, but to be able to look into the faces of my two biggest life accomplishments, my twin boys Dante and Dominic, and live my life to its fullest potential.

I am a parent and a woman who has been able to persevere in the midst of what was a massive shift in my life. It was time to go; it was my time to grow. I am grateful for the experience and knowledge the construction and development industry has given me. However, my life's blueprint was craving change and craving growth. It's scary at first, I have to admit, but once you surrender and trust in the process life has in store for you, it's a beautiful, rewarding experience. It's a recipe for growth, and it feels so empowering that you can taste it! It's better done with the right people to support you.

I am a blessed and fortunate woman. My ex-husband, Orlando, was my pivotal person. He made my dreams come true by helping me eliminate the obstacles I faced and supporting my decision to change the direction of my career. And with that being said, everything does happen for a reason. My life experiences, both the positive and negative ones, carved out who I am today. That's why I understand when my buyers are experiencing this growth of homeownership, this rollercoaster of emotions; I am their biggest fan and their pivotal person. I understand if the ones on the outside feel I do too much for my buyers, but that's their truth. I stand true to mine and I am forever grateful for the experiences in my life. Every buyer has inspired the messages on these pages and Homebuyer Rollercoaster is an imprint I leave on the world.

Chapter Three

HOME SWEET HOME

"Our only limitations are those we set up in our own minds."
– Napoleon Hill

You know you want to buy your home. You can see yourself living there. Sometimes you even dream it and feel it. But you're not sure of the steps to take that will get you there. I understand how buying your home can sometimes feel as if you're walking through a maze. There are many directions you can go, and you don't want to get lost in the process. You may feel confused and in need of guidance. So how can you make this happen so it's as painless as possible? I'll give you the answer: it's a plan. You always need a plan. This plan is created after I do my MRI and it's called the Buyer Blueprint. We will discuss the Buyer Blueprint in depth in the following chapter.

You're Not Alone

Traditional methods of real estate teach agents to prequalify buyers based on finances. Once they have what everyone refers to as a letter of prequalification from the bank, the agent and buyers go out looking for homes. If the buyer has issues pre-qualifying, they are turned away and told to come back once they are ready.

This never worked for me. I'm not saying that traditional methods don't work. I'm saying I created a way that works better for me where I see outstanding results.

Yes, I sell real estate. But what makes me different is that I take the time to connect and care. I do this through the MRI process. It's important that I not only ask critical questions but that I listen during the MRI. Anyone can hear your responses, but listening is a skill on its own. When I ask if you would prefer a two-story or one-story home? If you answer one-story this is what I hear. Is your choice because you have an elderly or disabled family member that cannot use stairs? If you do, do you prefer to be located near a hospital? Will you need to have extra funds to modify the home for handicap access? When I ask how many members in the family? You mention you have several children. My thoughts are: Male or female? Will they share a room? Any college age kids that may want extra privacy? When you use listening skills you dig deeper than what's on the surface, and this is not an interrogation but making a genuine connection with my buyer. I get to know the buyer's needs and wants both emotionally and financially. I meet with the family and understand their long-term goals. I connect with my buyers on a deeper level. They not only commit to working with me, but I also commit to working with them. Depending on each person's individual situation, I create your Blueprint. It may be a two-month, three-month, six-month, or eight-month Blueprint. This is not just a reflection of your financial situation, but it's part of your psychological and lifestyle assessment. If something occurs in your life that affects the goals we set out, we revise it and set new time frames. However, I will promise you that if you follow the original Blueprint that has been created just for you and you allow yourself to be coached, you will reach your goal.

There's Hope

Many times, I have buyers that I meet with and it goes something like this: "Okay, I want to buy, but … I'll be ready next year; I don't have enough money; I don't have a co-borrower; I have bad credit; my student loans and credit cards are too high; I'm waiting for my credit score to get to a 700; I'm planning my wedding; my lease is not up; I haven't finished school yet; I only have $5,000…" and my all-time favorite: "It's not meant to be."

What's your objection to getting what you want? People tend to self-sabotage. Not to say these feelings are not real, but they are a deflection. They're a way of justifying why something good isn't happening. It's human nature to get in our own way. I see all of these objections as having solutions; nothing I hear would hinder me from helping someone achieve their dream. Only you can get in your own way. Normally the buyers are the ones who give up on themselves, and this goes back to me wanting it more than they do. We just need the right person by our side to motivate us and walk us through one step at a time. That's why I'm a Buyer's Coach. I have faith in you when you have lost faith in yourself.

Belief System

Your mind is a powerful thing, and it was meant to create happiness and joy—not to do a disservice to you. We are raised with a belief system; however, beliefs can be changed. What you believe is what you will receive. Many of us have not been raised to think like successful people do. Did you know that successful people do not believe in procrastination? They believe in action.

The simple fact that you have picked up this book and have gotten this far into the chapters is because you believe, and you are taking action. You have already taken your first step. You are preparing yourself psychologically and emotionally by nourishing your brain. Many people get in the way of their own success. They are too much in their own head. Don't let your negative thoughts or beliefs get in the way.

I encourage my buyers to visualize themselves in their home and how it would be. How would life be different for them. How this would affect their lives and the lives of their children and loved ones. Connect with the feelings that bring you happiness. This is why it's important for me to connect with and assess my buyer psychologically and emotionally. I need to know where you are at, not only in your mind but in your heart. Sometimes even that needs calibration in order to be aligned with your Buyer Blueprint, which we will learn more about in Chapter Four. The process of homeownership is for those that are ready both in the heart and mind. I sign up to be part of your journey, and I also invest a little piece of myself with every buyer I represent because I believe.

Now we're going to take a closer look at one couple's homebuying journey. If you have been through a negative homebuying experience, you can know through the story of Sean and Sabrina that there is hope. When you least expect it, dreams do come true. When you may feel you need a miracle, miracles do happen.

New Beginnings: The Story of Sean and Sabrina

Sabrina was disillusioned and depleted from her experience with the homebuying process. She explained to me that she had made the final attempt to find the person that could help her finally buy her home. She didn't have the energy to be the one to contact me, as she was "done." She asked her fiancé Sean to call on their behalf and trusted him to decide if—depending on how our conversation went—she would give her dream of owning her own home one last shot or let it go.

Sean called and was very concerned, because he didn't want Sabrina to be let down again. He was very protective of her feelings. He shared Sabrina's feelings with me, explaining, "She's tired of dealing with realtors and tired of being told we can buy and then never getting approved. We've been told we don't have enough money or high enough credit scores after months of looking at homes. Realtors initially tell us it can happen, and it always ends up where we visualize ourselves in the home to only be told it was no longer going to be possible."

This is something I often hear from prospective buyers, and they are emotionally drained and put through an emotional rollercoaster. I understood what Sabrina was feeling, and I immediately connected with Sean.

I explained, "I'm very sorry this has been your experience and that you both have had to go through this, but I feel that you will be able to value what I have to offer since you have been through so much. There are no coincidences. We have met for a reason, and I promise you that if you still have just a spark left (which I know you do or you would not have reached out), and you can see yourselves hanging in there just a little bit longer, I promise not to let you down. If I feel this cannot happen, I will tell you what you need to do to make it happen. I will not waste your time or mine, but if I can make this dream come true for you, I will promise to treat you as if you were family. I will promise to protect you and guide you as if you were my family."

I knew Sean would connect with my sincerity and he responded, "We are in the middle of planning our destination wedding, and it will take place within a couple of months. It would be great if we would be able to move in by the time we are officially husband and wife."

In reality, Sabrina may have felt disillusioned by her journey, but I knew she was in a place of love and appreciation. Her wedding to the man she loved was around the corner. She still had a little bit of flame left in her, like a candle that was just flickering and flickering, about to go out. Her negative experience was there so that when something of value was presented to her, she would instantly recognize it. Through my connection with Sean, she would give it one more shot.

Sean and Sabrina came in to see me, we analyzed their situation together, and I made them part of each step of the process. That way they would not feel that they were in the dark, and they would understand and be able to ask questions and feel confident of the steps to follow. I'm a firm believer that when people know better they do better, and when people are educated they make better decisions for themselves and their family. I knew Sean and Sabrina needed the transparency. Soon enough their entire emotional state was in a place of gratitude and appreciation.

Now everything was in alignment again. I was able to rebuild her spark into a bright shining light. They had a few challenges where we needed to move around some assets and also get rid of liabilities. One of the biggest challenges they had was very high car payments. This was holding them back from being approved for their loan. Instead of turning them away until the car loan ended, we were able to turn in the car and swap it out for a new car with a lower payment. They also needed to pay off some debt. We were able to reach out to family to help them lower their debt enough to be within guidelines to obtain a mortgage loan.

Once these debts were paid down, their credit scores were higher, and Sean and Sabrina were ready to buy. They were part of the process, and they were once again full of hope and enthusiasm. I found Sean and Sabrina the home of their dreams, placed an offer, and it was accepted just in time. The wedding day came and then the honeymoon. Pictures of their special day were constantly coming into my cellphone inbox; I was so happy for them. All their dreams were coming true!

They felt our connection and they shared with me one of the most cherished milestones of their lives. Sabrina not only had the wedding of her dreams, but as soon as they returned from the honeymoon, Sean and Sabrina also closed on their home sweet home.

Chapter Four

HOMEBUYER BLUEPRINT

In this chapter we are going to talk about creating your Homebuyer Blueprint, which I cover in my Homebuyer Workshops and will help you understand the benefits of buying, use visualization techniques to reach your desired outcome, understand budgets for spending and saving, evaluate your credit, and much more. There are seven steps to the Homebuyer Blueprint, the first of which we will talk about is where you are today.

Step One: Let's Take a Look at Where You are Today

This step of the Homebuyer Blueprint is actually where you share where it is that you are emotionally in this process and how you got there. More of an open dialogue. It's important to know your story and how you and your family and anyone who's part of this purchase feels and what it is that drives you. When you look at your current living situation, how does it make you feel? Are you happy in the community you live in? The schools and neighborhood that affect your children? Are you tired of having to move every year because you're not happy with your landlord? Tired of requesting repairs that never get addressed? Is your environment and living situation making you feel as if you're about to lose your sanity? What has your homebuying experience been like? Have you tried to buy a home but just don't feel as if you have the proper guidance? What do you feel would have made this experience different? Do you feel as if you're going to be living this way for many more years? Have you been told repeatedly that you're not ready to qualify for a home loan? What do you wish you could change? Today, take a closer look at not only your current financial situation but how this rollercoaster of a homebuying process has affected you and your family emotionally. As a Buyer's Coach it's important that I not only look at the standard home loan qualifying requirements in order to properly guide you; but, to also connect with how this journey has impacted your state of mind. If you're just beginning the process, what are your expectations? Homebuying can at times make you feel as if you're losing your sanity. There are ups and downs and bumps in the road. The best way I can explain it is a rollercoaster ride. Just when you think you have passed the most challenging part, things take a turn for what may seem like the worst and before you can expect it, things take a turn to the complete opposite direction and before you know it, you are back up again, then slowly reaching the end of the ride. However, it's how we handle these moments that will determine our outcome. So many buyers give up their dream because of the emotional ride. What you may not realize is that nothing of value comes easy and the feeling of empowerment in owning your own home is not something the can be explained until you experience it. Repeatedly, buyers that reach the closing table tell me that they were so glad that I pushed them forward and didn't give up on them, because of the immense feeling of satisfaction they felt was something they could not have even dreamed of. So let's start by recognizing that reaching our dream is worth the ride.

Step Two: Calculate Your Rent

Now let's take a look at the first financial impact you have had so far. Many of you are renting. Do you know how much you have spent in rent in your lifetime? Let's do a calculation so we can have a better perspective of how much you have invested in someone else's mortgage. Ooh that hurts. Just saying it to you, hurts me. How many years have you been renting? Not in the property you are in currently in, but in the span of your life. Have you been renting five years, ten years, fifteen years of your life in total? Let's calculate this together.

For example: you have been renting for ten years with an average rental payment of $1,500 monthly. Each year has twelve months. $1,500 multiplied by twelve is $18,000. So yearly you have spent $18,000 in rent. Ten years multiplied by $18,000 is a total of $180,000 paid in rent to date. Yes $180,000 paid in rent. That is a lot of hard-earned money. Use this step by step formula to input your scenario to find out how much total rent you have paid in your lifetime:

Step One: $Average Rent Payment x 12 Months
= $Yearly Rent Paid

$ (Average Rent Amount)	X 12 (Months)	= $ (Yearly Rent Paid)

Step Two: $Yearly Rent Paid x Total Years Renting
= $Total Rent Paid to Date

$ (Yearly Amount)	X 10 (Years)	= $ (Lifetime Rent Paid)

This may be the first time you've looked at this number, or you already know your number. This number is your pain, your motivation to act. Look at this number because together we are going to turn this number into something that works for you instead of against you. That number will become your motivation to do better and make better life decisions. How do we make better life decisions? The most favorable outcomes are reached when we have a clear picture of where it is we are and what we want. We know as tenants we are not in a favorable financial position. We have no control over the space we live in. We have no stability or security as to what will happen the next lease renewal. If you will have to move? Will the landlord sell the property? We have no control over how much our housing costs will be year after year. Most importantly we are not gaining any equity and are paying someone else's mortgage.

Step Three: Benefits of Buying

There is no doubt that buying has the advantage of owning the most valuable asset that you will ever buy in life, your home. Do you know what the advantages are of buying a home?

Here are a few:

- Unlike a car which depreciates in value, a home appreciates over time
- You have control over your living space; paint walls or hang pictures wherever you wish
- Stable and predictable housing costs; no more rent raises each year
- Tax deduction on your interest and property taxes
- Gain equity and provide a nest egg for the future
- Sense of pride and empowerment
- Establish close ties with the community

Step Four: The Seven Steps to Visualize Your Desires

Time to play a game. It's called The Visualization Game. Visualization is a technique that will help you achieve your personal goals as you see them come to fruition in front of you. Your only limit is your own mind. Visualize when you're calm, focused and comfortable. This works better when you're at peace, free from immediate worries and at ease. Fewer distractions will make this process a lot easier.

Step One: Visualize the Result You Desire

Find a quiet, comfortable space. Close your eyes and begin to picture what your life would be like if you owned your own home. Start with the larger images. The house, the yard, the kitchen. How many bedrooms? Bathrooms? Then begin to scale down to the actual furniture, the flooring color, the drapes, décor. Imagine yourself inside your home. Who's with you? What are you wearing? What's going on in your home? Dinner? Watching a game with friends and family? Who's there? Imagine the family pictures on the walls. How do you feel in your home? What does it smell like? What's cooking in the kitchen? Start to open windows and smell the fresh air.

Step Two: Visualize with Positive Thoughts

Nothing will manifest if you feel you have no chance in life that it will happen. If you don't think it will work, it won't. So, for the duration of this exercise imagine that this is actually going to work. You have nothing to lose. Visualization is a sort of hypnosis. You have to allow it to work. Allow these desires to be part of your real life. So, incorporate what you visualized in step one with positive thoughts. Instead of picturing your home thinking, "It's a beautiful home but I can't imagine how this will happen." Think something like, "It's a beautiful home and I know I will find the way to be living in it within the next three months." Imagine the journey of you getting there to be an enjoyable one.

Step Three: Visualize this into the Real World

Now visualize your desired result for a few moments with as much detail and positive thoughts as possible. Until it brings you good feelings. Move it into the real world. Make changes in your real life to bring the goal to manifestation. Even if it's not tangible like "my home loan is approved," apply it to your everyday. Start budgeting your money. Maybe pay down a credit card or refrain from an unnecessary purchase that you may have acted upon normally. Visualize the phone ringing. Imagine receiving the call from the bank telling you you're approved for your mortgage loan. How does he sound? How do you feel when you hear his voice on the other end of the call?

Step Four: Think About the Events Needed to Reach Your Desired Goal

Imagine how you would get there and what steps you need to take. Big changes are comprised of small steps. If your desire is to be a homeowner: Imagine yourself meeting with your coach, gathering all your documents to meet with your lender, addressing issues on your credit report. How would that version of you handle these changes/situations?

Step Five: Visualize the Personality Traits You Need to Get You There

You want to be a homeowner, but what are the personality traits and qualities you need to get you there? Visualize yourself not just owning your home but the skills you need: open communication, patience, trust in the process, empowerment, listening, accepting expert advice, positivity. Imagine yourself communicating with the experts, open, positive, accepting of the process and trusting all will go your way.

Step Six: Apply Affirmations to Motivate Yourself

Pictures and phrases work very well. If you see yourself in your home with your family having dinner in the dining room with a beautifully decorated home, tell yourself, "I'm happy living with my family in my beautiful new home sharing dinner." Or, "My family and I live in a wonderful neighborhood in the home of our dreams." Cutting out pictures of what your home will look like and writing the affirmation behind it is also an option. You can do this for anything you desire in your life. Even a skill or task. "I am healthy and fit working out daily." Repeat these affirmations as much as needed.

Step Seven: Imagine Overcoming Setbacks

No one reaches success without encountering failure. Mistakes and setbacks are normal. It's how you bounce back that's more important than the setback itself. Obstacles are a normal part of life, without them we would not value where we are today. Adversity is a normal part of the journey. It's how you face the adversity that makes the difference, not that there was adversity to begin with. Ask yourself daily, "What can I do today to make myself better tomorrow?"

We all have a personal powerhouse. It's your gut instinct, and together with visualization, which is really a form of meditation, you can begin to connect and manifest everything you desire. In the beginning this will feel a bit funny, but if it doesn't you're not doing it right. Push past that foreign feeling, it does go away.

In my Homebuyer Workshops I cover "The Power of Visualization" in further detail and also in Chapter Nine with Goals and Affirmations, where you can actually use your visualization technique to produce results. You will learn to focus on long-term goals, be affirmative, create realistic goals, and start to visualize from your own first-person perspective as if you're seeing your future through your own eyes.

Practice this visualization technique for thirty-one days. It can be for as little as three minutes a day, at any time of the day, as many times as you feel you need it. You may also wish to journal your daily progress in the following pages. At the end of the thirty-one days how do you feel different?

JOURNAL
Day 1

_____

_____

_____

_____

_____

_____

_____

_____

_____

_____

_____

_____

_____

_____

_____

_____

_____

_____

_____

_____

JOURNAL
Day 2

_____

_____

_____

_____

_____

_____

_____

_____

_____

_____

_____

_____

_____

_____

_____

_____

_____

_____

_____

_____

_____

_____

JOURNAL
Day 3

JOURNAL
Day 4

_____

_____

_____

_____

_____

_____

_____

_____

_____

_____

_____

_____

_____

_____

_____

_____

_____

_____

_____

_____

JOURNAL
Day 5

_____
_____
_____
_____
_____
_____
_____
_____
_____
_____
_____
_____
_____
_____
_____
_____
_____
_____
_____
_____
_____

JOURNAL
Day 6

JOURNAL
Day 7

_____
_____
_____
_____
_____
_____
_____
_____
_____
_____
_____
_____
_____
_____
_____
_____
_____
_____
_____
_____
_____
_____
_____
_____
_____

JOURNAL
Day 8

_____

_____

_____

_____

_____

_____

_____

_____

_____

_____

_____

_____

_____

_____

_____

_____

_____

_____

_____

_____

_____

_____

JOURNAL
Day 9

_____

_____

_____

_____

_____

_____

_____

_____

_____

_____

_____

_____

_____

_____

_____

_____

_____

_____

_____

_____

_____

JOURNAL
Day 10

_____

_____

_____

_____

_____

_____

_____

_____

_____

_____

_____

_____

_____

_____

_____

_____

_____

_____

_____

_____

JOURNAL
Day 11

JOURNAL
Day 12

_____

_____

_____

_____

_____

_____

_____

_____

_____

_____

_____

_____

_____

_____

_____

_____

_____

_____

_____

_____

_____

JOURNAL
Day 13

_____

_____

_____

_____

_____

_____

_____

_____

_____

_____

_____

_____

_____

_____

_____

_____

_____

_____

_____

_____

_____

_____

JOURNAL
Day 14

_____
_____
_____
_____
_____
_____
_____
_____
_____
_____
_____
_____
_____
_____
_____
_____
_____
_____
_____
_____
_____
_____

JOURNAL
Day 15

_____

_____

_____

_____

_____

_____

_____

_____

_____

_____

_____

_____

_____

_____

_____

_____

_____

_____

_____

_____

_____

_____

_____

JOURNAL
Day 16

_____
_____
_____
_____
_____
_____
_____
_____
_____
_____
_____
_____
_____
_____
_____
_____
_____
_____
_____

JOURNAL
Day 17

_____

_____

_____

_____

_____

_____

_____

_____

_____

_____

_____

_____

_____

_____

_____

_____

_____

_____

_____

_____

_____

JOURNAL
Day 18

JOURNAL
Day 19

_____
_____
_____
_____
_____
_____
_____
_____
_____
_____
_____
_____
_____
_____
_____
_____
_____
_____
_____
_____
_____
_____

JOURNAL
Day 20

JOURNAL
Day 21

_____
_____
_____
_____
_____
_____
_____
_____
_____
_____
_____
_____
_____
_____
_____
_____
_____
_____
_____
_____
_____
_____
_____
_____
_____

JOURNAL
Day 22

_____
_____
_____
_____
_____
_____
_____
_____
_____
_____
_____
_____
_____
_____
_____
_____
_____
_____
_____
_____
_____
_____

JOURNAL
Day 23

_____

_____

_____

_____

_____

_____

_____

_____

_____

_____

_____

_____

_____

_____

_____

_____

_____

_____

_____

_____

_____

_____

JOURNAL
Day 24

_____
_____
_____
_____
_____
_____
_____
_____
_____
_____
_____
_____
_____
_____
_____
_____
_____
_____
_____
_____
_____
_____
_____

JOURNAL
Day 25

_____
_____
_____
_____
_____
_____
_____
_____
_____
_____
_____
_____
_____
_____
_____
_____
_____
_____
_____
_____
_____

JOURNAL
Day 26

_____

_____

_____

_____

_____

_____

_____

_____

_____

_____

_____

_____

_____

_____

_____

_____

_____

_____

_____

_____

_____

_____

_____

JOURNAL
Day 27

_____
_____
_____
_____
_____
_____
_____
_____
_____
_____
_____
_____
_____
_____
_____
_____
_____
_____
_____
_____
_____
_____
_____
_____
_____

JOURNAL
Day 28

_____
_____
_____
_____
_____
_____
_____
_____
_____
_____
_____
_____
_____
_____
_____
_____
_____
_____
_____
_____
_____

JOURNAL
Day 29

_____

_____

_____

_____

_____

_____

_____

_____

_____

_____

_____

_____

_____

_____

_____

_____

_____

_____

_____

_____

_____

_____

_____

JOURNAL
Day 30

_____
_____
_____
_____
_____
_____
_____
_____
_____
_____
_____
_____
_____
_____
_____
_____
_____
_____
_____
_____
_____

JOURNAL
Day 31

Step Five: Budgeting

Part of becoming a homeowner is learning how to manage your money responsibly. The worksheet below will help you take a look at your current finances to determine how much should you save and how much you can spend. This can give you an idea of what it will take to save for your down payment and closing costs. Similar to rent payments, it's necessary to take a look every so often at where our money goes so we can determine if we need to shift expenses in order to reach our goals. Creating a budget is necessary in order to be able to allocate funds as we prioritize for homeownership lifestyle. Let's take a look at how financially healthy you are.

Determining the Amount You Can Save:

Monthly income:

- What is your monthly take-home pay? $ _____
- What is your spouse's or partner's monthly take-home pay? $ _____
- How much money do you receive each month from other sources? $ _____
- How much have you and your spouse or partner saved already? $ _____

What's your Total Monthly Income? $ _____

Monthly bills and expenses:

- Do you have spousal or child support obligations? What are they? $ _____

- How much is your monthly rent? $ _____
- What is your monthly car payment(s)? $ _____
- What is your current student loan
  payment(s)? $ _____

What is your total monthly payment
for all your credit cards? *$* _____

How much do you currently spend each month for:

- Electricity $ _____
- Gas (your heating/cooling bill) $ _____
- Telephone service $ _____
- Cable/satellite service $ _____
- Water and sewer service $ _____
- Renter's insurance (divide the yearly
  premium by twelve) $ _____
- Groceries and household supplies $ _____
- Clothing $ _____
- Health club dues $ _____
- Other fees or dues $ _____
- Fuel and repairs for your car $ _____
- Books, movies, video rentals, dining
  out, etc. $ _____
- The lottery and other incidental
  purchases $ _____

What's your Total Monthly Payments
& Spending? *$* _____

Now calculate your leftover cash

- Enter your total monthly income from
  the calculation above $ _____
- Enter your **total monthly payments
  and spending** calculated above $ _____
- Subtract the second figure from the first $ _____

What's your total? $ _____

WORKBOOK

_____
_____
_____
_____
_____
_____
_____
_____
_____
_____
_____
_____
_____
_____
_____
_____
_____
_____
_____
_____
_____
_____

WORKBOOK

_____

_____

_____

_____

_____

_____

_____

_____

_____

_____

_____

_____

_____

_____

_____

_____

_____

_____

_____

_____

_____

_____

WORKBOOK

_____
_____
_____
_____
_____
_____
_____
_____
_____
_____
_____
_____
_____
_____
_____
_____
_____
_____
_____
_____
_____
_____
_____
_____
_____
_____

WORKBOOK

_____

_____

_____

_____

_____

_____

_____

_____

_____

_____

_____

_____

_____

_____

_____

_____

_____

_____

_____

_____

_____

_____

WORKBOOK

_____
_____
_____
_____
_____
_____
_____
_____
_____
_____
_____
_____
_____
_____
_____
_____
_____
_____
_____
_____
_____
_____
_____
_____

WORKBOOK

_____
_____
_____
_____
_____
_____
_____
_____
_____
_____
_____
_____
_____
_____
_____
_____
_____
_____
_____
_____
_____
_____
_____
_____
_____

WORKBOOK

_____

_____

_____

_____

_____

_____

_____

_____

_____

_____

_____

_____

_____

_____

_____

_____

_____

_____

_____

_____

_____

_____

_____

WORKBOOK

_____

_____

_____

_____

_____

_____

_____

_____

_____

_____

_____

_____

_____

_____

_____

_____

_____

_____

_____

_____

_____

WORKBOOK

_____

_____

_____

_____

_____

_____

_____

_____

_____

_____

_____

_____

_____

_____

_____

_____

_____

_____

_____

_____

_____

_____

_____

_____

WORKBOOK

_____

_____

_____

_____

_____

_____

_____

_____

_____

_____

_____

_____

_____

_____

_____

_____

_____

_____

_____

_____

_____

After taking a look at your results: Do you need to reprioritize? Do you need to shift expenses? Many times, we can cut down on things that can help us save more money than we are saving right now with just some basic changes. Where can you make changes? Here are some tips for saving money for a down payment and closing costs:

- Put away credit cards, only spend the money you have on hand
- Limit spending on entertainment
- Start a home saving account and contribute a portion from every paycheck
- Track daily expenses
- Save your tax refund
- Skip vacations for the year
- Reduce any high interest rate credit cards
- Generate more income by additional work hours or a second job
- Reduce household expenses

Now that you have a better idea of where your financial health is, keep saving! There's more than one way of gathering funds for your down payment and closing costs. Let's take a look at other options that you can use for down payment:

- Receiving a gift from a family member
- Down payment assistance programs
- 401K hardship withdrawal or loan

How much money did you determine you could borrow? Now that you have a better understanding of how you can save for your down payment, know that different kinds of mortgages require different down payments. The more money you have to put down, the more advantageous terms you can get for your mortgage contract. However, lenders are very willing to sell you a mortgage with a low-down payment, too. To get an idea of what your down payment might be multiply the amount you'd like to borrow or the purchase price by 3.5%, 5%, 10% and 20%. For example a $345,000 home purchase would look like this:

Purchase Price $345,000 x 0.035 = $12,075
Purchase Price $345,000 x 0.050 = $17,250
Purchase Price $345,000 x 0.10 = $34,500
Purchase Price $345,000 x 0.20 = $69,000

Calculating closing costs will give you a rough idea of how much it will cost to complete your purchase. There's also more than one way for gathering funds for your closing costs. Let's take a look at options for closing costs:

- Seller Contribution
- Lender Credit

How much money did you determine in contribution and credits? There are different guidelines on how much a seller can contribute depending on the type of mortgage loan. FHA loans allow up to a six percent seller contribution. Conventional loans allow up to a three percent seller contribution. Depending on the market not all sellers are willing to contribute to closing costs, however three-six percent depending on the loan is the allowable amount. One way to be able to receive a closing costs contribution from a seller is by buying a new construction home. Many developers offer seller contributions toward closing costs as an incentive to help make homeownership possible for buyers. Estimate seller contribution by the purchase price as done in the example above. Closing costs are estimated to be about two-five percent of your loan amount. Estimate closing costs by multiplying your loan amount (the amount being financed) first by 2% and then by 5%, see example below of a $320,000 loan amount:

Loan Amount $320,000 x 0.02 = $6,400
Loan Amount $320,000 x 0.05 = $16,000

Step Six: Evaluate your Credit

Many people take their credit for granted. Until they are shopping for a home mortgage loan when they realize what a big impact credit can have on their future purchase. If you are purchasing a home and need to acquire a mortgage loan, credit may be one of the most important factors, if not the backbone of your loan. Being aware of the state of your financial health includes the state of your credit score and the information on your credit report. It can impact the type of loan you qualify for, your interest rate and mortgage insurance to name a few. Different loan programs require different credit scores. The FHA loan program allows you to qualify with a credit score as low as 580. Conventional loans require a minimum of 620. Monitoring your credit is always strongly suggested. Not only to prepare for your home purchase but to also protect yourself from misuse of your credit or identity theft. There are many monitoring systems available. It's recommended to use a system that gives you your scores from the three credit bureaus and has the option of showing you the scoring model for a mortgage loan. Your credit scores may be very different depending on the scoring model. Shopping for a car loan vs. home loan will have very different scoring results. A monitoring system that offers a variety of scoring models including the mortgage loan model is www.myfico.com. Here are a few things that can hurt your credit score:

- Paying credit cards late or not paying at all
- High credit card balances
- Closing credit card accounts with available credit or old credit
- Maxed out or over the limit credit card balances
- Hard inquiries or opening new credit
- Late car payment
- Late mortgage payment
- Collections
- Delinquent student loans
- Judgements
- Foreclosure
- Bankruptcy

This may seem discouraging if your scores are not where they need to be at the moment, however creating your Homebuyer Blueprint will include target dates for credit repair in order to get you ready to purchase by a specified date. Many times it may seem overwhelming, but I'm here to tell you not to let this discourage you, everything has a solution. I have worked with buyers that have come to me with scores in the mid to upper 400s to low 500s, and as long they follow their Blueprint they make it to a successful closing. Depending what's on the credit report I have been able to raise their score a substantial amount of points in a relatively short time frame. Most cases can take from ninety days to six months. Once we know what your credit scores are and what's on your report we can then create your plan.

Step Seven: Buyer Blueprint Personalized

Your Buyer Blueprint is finalized by personalizing it to your situation. This includes mapping your personal finances at a much deeper level. As explained above credit is one of the many factors that impact your Blueprint, as well as your income, desired location, purchase price, whether or not there's a homeowner's association, property taxes, property insurance, current debts, and many other factors that I cover in my one-on-one meetings. We can discuss all this along with your current mindset and expectations in a private setting or my Homebuyer Workshops. The above exercises help me better understand where you are financially and emotionally and gives me the ability to create a roadmap to your success. This can be modified if something occurs that can throw you off track from your original timeline. The key to success is having a plan and a coach that makes sure that you do not allow your emotions to get the better of you. A coach that believes in you, pushes you forward and doesn't allow you to let your dream go. I'm honored to be part of this journey, rollercoaster and all. It's a milestone in your life like no other. It's one of the most memorable experiences you will ever have in your life. I still remember the day I purchased my first property. I remember exactly the day and time, how it all came to fruition. But most of all I remember how it made me feel. My wish for you is that you too can experience this unimaginable sense of pride.

Chapter Five

INITIAL REQUIREMENTS
OF BUYING A HOME

The process of buying your dream home may be challenging but it's a beautiful journey that you will eventually appreciate. You will make some really big decisions in your life, but none will be as memorable and emotional as buying your first home. It's euphoric feelings of independence and empowerment. It's the moment that you find the one, and it's an instant connection. The moment you receive those keys in your hands, it's like receiving keys to your temple. You never forget how fulfilled you felt the first time you walked into your first home. Let's take this chapter to introduce the practical side of the process and some of the questions that may have you feeling overwhelmed.

How Much Can I Afford?

You have made your decision to buy your home, and you're excited to start shopping. It's important to know how much you qualify for. However, depending on your situation, it's important that you are matched with the correct lending institution. Both lenders and banks loan money. The main differences between the two is that banks are a depository, so they will require you to open a bank account. They have stricter guidelines to approve a loan. Lenders are not depository; their guidelines are more flexible.

So, the real question is not "How much do I qualify for?" but "What institution is the right match for me?" Once you find the right match and your loan is approved, it feels like winning the lottery.

Down Payment Requirements

You found your dream home and your offer has been accepted. You are so excited that you're jumping with joy! In order for a contract to be legally binding, a monetary exchange is required.

What this means is that there will need to be a deposit placed in an escrow account. An escrow account is where your money is held by a third party, typically an attorney or a title company. They are there to make sure everything during the closing goes smoothly and they protect all the relevant parties by ensuring that no funds and property changes hands until all conditions in the purchase agreement have been met.

The total amount of down payment that you will required to bring the day of your closing depends on the loan type you're approved for. You can buy with less than a twenty percent down payment. There are many options which I will talk about in a bit more detail in Chapter Six: Other People's Money, and which we touched upon lightly in Chapter Four.

Credit Worthiness

Credit is important, but it's not a reason to hold you back from purchasing. You do not need to have a 700 credit score to buy. Yes, the higher the credit the better your interest rate. However, there are many ways to raise your score in a very short period of time.

But this is also something that we need to set in motion and something I discuss in my initial meeting and as part of the Homebuyer Blueprint. I have had buyers turned away from banks/lenders because they have been told by their credit simulators that the buyers score won't go up for another year. That same buyer closed within two months of being denied with another lender. That was Miranda from The Story of Michael and Miranda in Chapter Two. I raised her credit fifty-five points in four weeks as she was under contract, just in time to close.

Most banks and lenders shy away from buyers who have credit challenges because these are high maintenance files; they take up a lot of time and time is money. Aside from that, not everyone has knowledge in this field.

I welcome them. These are the files that are the most rewarding. It's another building block to me and they are very rewarding because you develop strong relationships with the buyers. These files are the ones I like to call the "ICU," because your credit may need intensive care and that's okay.

Income

Many buyers are not aware of the many options that exist to qualify for a home mortgage loan. Income is calculated many ways and there are many sources of income, not just your salary or hourly wages. If you receive disability income, alimony, overtime, supplemental security income or "SSI," or child support (to name a few) these may be used to qualify as income. In addition, you may add co-borrowers and non-occupant co-borrowers.

What Are Closing Costs?

Typically, homebuyers will pay closing costs estimated at two to five percent of the purchase price of the home. Closing costs also include prepays or prepaid items and are all the fees associated with buying a home. Some of those fees may include loan origination fees, discount points, appraisal fees, title searches, surveys, taxes, deed-recording fees, credit report charges, and many more. The good news about closing costs and prepays is that you as a buyer can get from three to six percent of these fees paid for as a seller contribution.

Can I Do This on My Own?

Sure, you can do this on your own, just as if you have a court case you can represent yourself. But are you going to have the outcome that you want? Are you well protected? Are you putting yourself in a strong negotiating position? Do you have the tools and expertise necessary to negotiate a contract? Do you have access to closed sales in the area to be able to present to the bank if the appraisal does not come in at value? Can you navigate through the extensive paperwork that's required to purchase a home? Can you interpret a purchase contract and its legal ramifications? In summary, if you want the best outcome with the least obstacles, leave it up to the professionals in this field to look after your best interest. This is what they do every day. They are familiar with the market and changes. They have relationships with colleagues and speak the same language. They have years of experience making them experts in the industry.

Do I Need a Realtor?

You don't need a realtor but having one can streamline this process. Purchasing a home can be a complicated and intimidating process at times. It's important to have someone on your team that's looking out for your best interest and acts as a support system and confidant. Your realtor can remove themselves from the emotional aspect of the transaction, because they are licensed professionals trained to present their clients in their best light when negotiating and agree to hold your information confidential. An agent's success is based on referrals not on one transaction but the ability to create long-term relationships making sure their clients are happy. This assures you that you will receive a service that is free and to your benefit, because a buyer's agent's commission is paid by the seller. So, take advantage if you're a buyer!

Chapter Six

OTHER PEOPLE'S MONEY

There are many myths about money in the homebuying process. By myths I mean information that has been carried over from generations ago. Like the twenty percent down rule or the 700 credit score. Buy smart, follow your intuition, and reach a higher level of homebuying wisdom. Other People's Money gives you the upper hand in financing options. The American Dream is about making it happen. In other countries, you are required to pay cash or put a minimum of fifty percent down payment. There are homeowners I have helped buy with just $5,000, using a combination of the loan programs discussed below. There are many different types of combinations to borrow funds. This takes an expert in the industry to help you add value to your homebuying experience.

Below are the essentials that allow you to invest less of your own funds while leveraging off of "OPM."

Down Payment Options

Saving up is hard, and one of the most common misconceptions that turns away buyers is the amount of down payment necessary to buy a home. The twenty percent down payment rule for decades was standard, but it isn't always the case anymore. There are many programs that allow you to buy with much less than twenty percent as not everyone can qualify for a conventional loan. FHA loans require three-and-a-half percent down payment for qualified first-time homebuyers. There are many down payment assistance programs that, if you qualify, may offer up to $15,000 and many can be combined with other monies.

Everything is Timing

As a buyer, you spend a lot of time looking through listings and going to visit homes you may consider. Waiting to find that one home that stands out among the rest, the one that as you walk through the door you can envision yourself in. You look through dozens of pictures trying to find the right floor plan. The most functional kitchen. The largest master bedroom or the perfect backyard.

In reality, what is going to make your decision is how you feel when you open the doors and pass the threshold. That moment when you find it, you will know it, and feel it in your entire being. In today's market, if you love the house and you can feel it, don't leave without putting an offer because someone else will. If you remember anything in this book, remember these last two sentences.

Grants and Bonds

There are many grants and bond loans that offer down payment assistance, but there are requirements to obtain down payment assistance such as credit, income, demographics, and home price. But just know that they are available and designed to make homebuying possible.

Closing Costs Paid

In Chapter Four, I spoke about closing costs and what they consisted of. These are costs that are inevitable; however, there are guidelines within the lending industry that allow for closing costs contributions. You may be asking, "What does this mean?" This means that a seller is allowed to pay up to six percent of the purchase price in closing costs on your behalf on an FHA loan.

Here's a brief example: Your purchase price is $345,000. To purchase this home, you would be required to have a down payment of three-and-a-half percent ($12,075), plus closing costs at five percent ($17,250). A total of $29,325 is needed to buy this house. If the seller agrees to contribute, up to six percent of purchase price, ($20,700) is allowable. This means that now you can invest your money into the down payment of the home or pure equity, which in turn will lower your monthly mortgage. Or you have the option of only paying the down payment of three-and-a-half percent or $12,075.

This example is just so you have an idea of how this works, but it's a bit more complex. The lender will guide you and explain what's the best scenario for you. In an active market, it may be difficult to find sellers that are willing to contribute to closing costs simply because they have no need to as they have multiple offers on a home. In this type of market and whenever you wish to request seller paid contributions its best left to the professionals to navigate those waters on your behalf.

100 Percent Financing

If you are a Veteran and submit your certificate of eligibility, you are entitled to receive one hundred percent financing, a zero-down payment, and one of the many benefits is that you are not required to pay mortgage insurance. Another benefit is that if you are eighty percent disabled, you are not required to pay property taxes on your loan. FHA also offers programs with one hundred percent financing.

Retirement Funds

Most buyers are not aware that they can buy with their retirement funds/401K without being penalized. Purchasing your first home with your retirement funds is not a loan but a hardship withdrawal. The amount you can request to withdraw as a hardship depends on your plan. It's a very simple process and usually takes about seven to ten days to have the funds transferred into your bank account.

Gifts

Gift Money is another source of funds that is permitted for primary and secondary home purchases. They require a gift letter signed by the donor which states:

- Donor's contact information
- The dollar amounts
- Donor's signature
- Donor's relationship to buyer
- Date funds were transferred
- Statement that no repayment is expected
- Address of property being purchased

In addition, the donor may be required to provide a bank statement. The donor can be a close friend or family.

Chapter Seven

WHAT'S "THE" BIG DEAL?

Your search is finally over, you have finally found the home of your dreams, and you have found "The One." You have seen it a few times by now. The contract has been accepted by the seller, and all you can do is imagine the day you move in. You have gone through the loan process and your loan is finally approved! You receive your "Clear to Close," and it feels like Christmas. You're a step closer to the home of your dreams. You can feel it; you wake up every morning waiting for the day when you're in your new home. You envision yourself walking through the front doors, and the first time you enter the kitchen you can imagine your first family dinner together. A sense of peace consumes you because you can already feel the security and stability owning your own home can bring. You are at the finish line, and it's the last stretch. What can go wrong?

Debt-to-Income Ratios or "DTI" is one of the major factors in obtaining a loan. There are two types:

- **Front-End Ratio** is made up of all costs associated with a mortgage, not including your other debts. Sometimes it's also referred to as a **Housing-to-Income Ratio**. Housing expenses are your estimated monthly mortgage payment, homeowner's insurance, HOA fees, and property taxes. To figure your front-end ratio, take your mortgage payment ($1,500) and divide it by your monthly income ($5,000) for a total front-end DTI ratio of thirty percent.

- **Back-End Ratio** uses the amount of a borrower's total debt payments, not just the mortgage payment. Debt payments are any loans or lines of credit you pay on monthly. These include: auto loans, credit card minimum payments, student loans, personal loans, and child support. To figure your back-end ratio, you need to add up all of your monthly payments and include your estimated mortgage payment and divide it by your gross pre-tax income.

Opening up new lines of credit would not be a good idea prior to closing. Most buyers don't know that their credit is being watched not only after the loan is approved but until the very day of closing. The lender will recheck your credit even after your loan is approved and you receive your "Clear to Close."

Change of employment can become a very big issue, even if you make the same amount of money or more in this new job. You may think, "Well, what's the difference?" The lender will call your old employer and verify your job on the very day of closing, and if you're no longer there, it's going to be a huge issue. Your new job needs to be verified and pay-stubs need to be turned in. This late in the process, it could cause a delay and your deposit may be at risk. Lenders like to see stability with the same conditions that existed at the time of the loan approval. They want to see that you are financially stable and capable of making your loan payments. Unless it's completely necessary to make the job switch without notification, it's best to keep open lines of communication with your lender and Realtor Coach and notify him/her before making the move.

Purchasing furniture or any big-ticket item can be quite tempting as you are making plans to move in to your new home. Even if the furniture store line of credit offers a deferred payment until next year the lender assumes you will be making that new monthly payment immediately and will more than likely affect your DTI ratio. If you need new furniture for your home, wait until after closing and the keys are in your hands.

Lending your credit will directly affect you. For example, if you lend your credit to someone for the purchase of a car, even if you're not the primary person and act as the co-signer, the bank still assumes you are financially responsible, and this too will more than likely affect your DTI ratio. It also reflects a hard credit check in your credit. If you are thinking of becoming a co-signer, wait until your loan closes.

Missing a payment on any of your accounts, whether it's on a car payment, credit card, or student loan, will cause your credit to be flagged. When the Lender finds out (and they will), this can cause you to lose your loan.

Keep your car. We all want to improve our life, and through the excitement of buying our new home we start to want to improve other things. We feel we are on top of the world, and a car at the top of the list is the most common change and mistake that homebuyers make. Not only does it reflect a hard credit check on your report, but in most cases multiple credit checks must occur, since car dealers usually submit your application to various banks. In most cases, adding that new additional monthly payment throws off your ratios and also your home loan. Be careful if you're thinking of buying yourself a car, because it may be the one thing driving you away from your dream home.

Protect your savings or the money you have for closing costs. Set these funds aside and pretend they are not there. Many buyers are tempted to use these monies and they become hard to recover. It's tempting but try to avoid spending it.

Applying for additional loans not only affects your DTI ratio, but most importantly your credit score. Buyers make the mistake of thinking that since the new home loan is approved, the new credit won't be seen until after closing. Mistakenly enough that's not guaranteed, and your new home loan can fall through in the final stages.

Increasing or closing credit cards. Even if you realize you never use a certain card, do not cancel that credit line. Store the card away or cut it into pieces. If you're thinking of buying a new washer and dryer on credit for your home, it can wait. Your credit needs to remain the same as when your lender pulled it on the day of your approval. On the other hand, if your DTI ratio is high, then paying down credit cards may be a good idea. It's important to consult this with your lender and Real Estate Coach prior to using any funds you may have saved.

You may be saying to yourself, "What's the big deal?" What makes sense and seems obvious to you is looked at very differently in the eyes of the lender. The lending process has drastically changed since generations ago. Lenders are much more cautious about who they give loans to. They like to see stability and that you maintain the same conditions as when your loan was approved. Any additional changes like the ones discussed above reflect as instability. Don't underestimate the process of obtaining a loan. The lender will be extremely thorough in their evaluation. It's important to have a strong connection between yourself, your lender, and your Real Estate Coach. You have an experienced team of professionals behind you, all working toward the same goal. Trust in the process and be sure to follow the plan. This is "*The*" big deal.

Chapter Eight
WHAT'S NEXT?

You are finally under contract. Now what do you do? How do you know what your mortgage payment will be on this home? What does your mortgage payment cover? These are only some of the questions you may have. Your realtor will forward the executed contract to your lender, so you can start the application for your mortgage loan.

Here is an overview of the steps coming up until closing:

Loan Estimate is a three-page form you receive after applying for a loan. The form uses clear language and is designed to help you better understand the terms of the mortgage loan you've applied for. When you receive a Loan Estimate, the lender has not yet approved or denied your loan application. The Loan Estimate shows you what loan terms the lender expects to offer if you decide to move forward. The form provides you with important information, including the estimated interest rate, monthly payment, and total closing costs for the loan. The Loan Estimate also gives you information about the estimated costs of taxes and insurance, and how the interest rate and payments may change in the future. In addition, the form indicates if the loan has special features that you will want to be aware of, like penalties for paying off the loan early (prepayment penalties).

Home Inspections are a vital part of the process. It's an inexpensive way to discover the conditions of the property and if any major repairs will be needed either immediately or in the future. This way you can make a better-informed decision on whether or not to make this purchase. I like to tell my buyers to look at this as a checklist of things to come, not to use an inspection as a negotiating tool. If you are buying a home that has a prior owner, there will always be about two percent in repairs. Most sellers are willing to make minor repairs prior to closing if requested. Unless the inspection uncovers major damage, like structural defects or a roof with no life expectancy, have your Realtor Coach renegotiate terms with seller. In addition, at this stage in the process contract terms allow you to walk away from the purchase with no penalties or risk of losing your deposit, as long as your Realtor Coach notifies the seller in writing within the stated number of days as per contract.

The appraisal is a vital and inevitable part of buying a home for anyone who needs a mortgage. It's the determination of the value of the home by a third party, a licensed and trained appraiser. An appraisal is important because it protects your investment by ensuring that you as the buyer do not pay more than what the home is worth based on comparable sales in the area. This is a very critical point, and it's important that your realtor is knowledgeable in area sales and negotiation. If the value comes in other than the purchase price, here is where the expertise come in. Don't allow your emotions to get the best of you; always maintain a positive mindset. There are resolutions, and your Real Estate Coach will negotiate new terms with the seller. This may include the seller reducing the purchase price, the buyer paying more, or both parties coming to a middle ground.

Final Loan Approval is determined by a professional "underwriter." This is an employee of the lender who approves or denies the loan by looking at all the supporting documentation and determines your level of risk. By the time you reach this stage, you have already been through the underwriting process and received a "**Conditional Approval.**" Now additional documentation to clear the conditions are submitted back to underwriting, and many times additional documentation is requested. Most buyers can become a bit impatient and annoyed by the request for documents. However, it's important to keep in mind that in reality the one buying the property is really the bank. In an FHA loan where the buyer buys with three-and-a-half percent down payment, the bank is taking the ninety-six-and-a-half percent risk on the balance of the purchase. Certain guidelines for obtaining a loan are required, so be patient and cooperate. The process will be much less stressful. An experienced Realtor Coach can assist in helping you gather documents.

Mortgage insurance is required and included in your monthly mortgage payment if you are giving less than twenty percent down payment on your house. This is an insurance policy you are required to pay to protect the lender from defaults on your mortgage. The amount is driven by your credit score, loan type, and down payment. FHA loans require an upfront Mortgage Insurance Premium (MIP), and it is for the life of the loan and can be removed by refinancing. Conventional loans have no upfront Premium Mortgage Insurance (PMI) and can be removed once you have at least twenty percent equity in the home by contacting the escrow department and requesting an appraisal to confirm your home value.

Property Insurance is required if you finance your home. This provides protection against most risks to the property, such as fire, theft, and windstorm damage. It can also help protect your belongings and personal items. This payment will be included in your monthly mortgage payment. In order to close, you will have to have property insurance quotes ready. If you are in a flood zone, an elevation certificate will be provided by the lender in order to obtain flood insurance quotes.

Closing Costs, Prepaid Items or "Prepaids," and Escrows are all the expenses and fees associated with the purchase of a home. They are typically two to five percent of the purchase price. These costs may include loan origination fees, discount points, appraisal fees, title searches, title insurance, surveys, taxes, deed-recording fees, and credit report charges. **Prepaid Items** are those that recur over time, such as property taxes and homeowners' insurance. These costs are required; however, there's always a silver lining, and the good news is there are loan programs that allow a seller contribution of three to six percent toward these costs. FHA allows six percent. In addition, if you are paying your insurance premium and property taxes through an escrow account, you'll need to include a couple months' worth of those payments to build up that account. **Escrow** is an account where the lender holds money to pay property taxes and insurance.

Clear to Close or CTC is the phone call we all wait for! It's when we can all have a sigh of relief. I say all that because by this point the loan officer and Realtor Coach, along with yourself the buyer, have put many hours of work into making this dream come true. A CTC is the news we have been waiting for: the lender's way of saying, "This is going to happen; we are almost at the finish line!" The underwriter has approved all documentation necessary for the title company to schedule the closing and start drafting the Closing Disclosure.

Then there's **TILA/RESPA Integrated Disclosure Rule**, also known as TRID. This rule is designed to help borrowers understand the terms of their home financing transaction, so there is a trend to start referring to this rule as the *Know Before You Owe Rule* instead of TRID. First, you will see consumer disclosures that are very easy to read. The Loan Estimate forms will clearly set forth the terms of the proposed transaction to help the borrower determine whether they would like to proceed with the transaction.

Closing Disclosure will be given to you next (at least three days prior to closing), so if there are any questions, you will be provided with additional information. This document gives you more details about your loan, its key terms, and how much you are paying in fees and other costs to get your mortgage and buy your home. It provides a breakdown of all the closing cost details and lists all loan costs and other costs paid by borrower, seller, and any other parties involved in the transaction.

Cash to Close is the monies required to bring on the big day when you'll hand over a cashier's check to cover your "cash to close," or the amount in exchange for the keys to your new home. The amount of cash you need to bring to closing includes down payment plus closing costs and prepaid items.

Attorney Representation for any part of a real estate transaction is optional. The legal fees for the closing attorney are one of several closing costs a homebuyer is responsible for paying at closing. Depending on the lender, buyers sometimes have a choice of whether they will hire the same attorney to represent both their lender and them.

Funding occurs the day you sign the papers and the bank funds your loan and you wire the amount of money you need at closing. Then you will be handed the keys and will finally be able to take possession of the home!

Keys are finally in your hands. You are now a homeowner ready to move in. This is the moment you have been waiting for! You have made it to the grand finale! All the papers have been signed, and the loan has been funded.

Chapter Nine

THE MENTAL GAME

"Believe in what you want so much that it has no choice but to materialize."

– Karen Salmansohn

Letting Your Mind Get the Best of You

The decision to buy a home comes as a new experience for many of us. You may not know what to expect, and many times you may feel as if you are lost in this process. There's the feeling of the unknown and the uncertainty of what comes next. Each step is new, but also a step closer toward your dream home. This may be one of the most important decisions you make in your lifetime. This can cause much stress and anxiety. You may even find yourself obsessing over the what-ifs.

We cannot always control the feelings we have, but we can control how we react to them. There is a way of controlling which direction your mind takes. Rather than being controlled by your emotions, you get to decide if your mind will be filled with negative or positive thoughts. You can do this by accepting the feelings and letting go of the thoughts that don't serve you. This way you can actually control your mind instead of having it control you. You can decide how this experience will be for you. Letting go is not about giving up but gaining control. Letting go starts with mindfulness, being aware of your thoughts, and what others are going through. Whatever situation you find yourself in, it is about having perspective.

Power of Visualization

For decades top performers, athletes, motivational speakers, high achievers, and the super-wealthy have uses visualization techniques to visualize their desired outcomes and reach their goals with razor sharp focus and powerful confidence to carve out the life of their dreams. We all have it in us already. We just need to bring it into our daily practice to accelerate our dreams and goals. Here are some benefits of activating visualization:

- You start to instantly recognize the tools you need to achieve your goals and dreams
- You activate the part of your subconscious that starts generating creativity to achieve goals

- It activates the Law of Attraction, tapping into more of the now and less of the what-if, drawing in positivity
- It stimulates motivation to act to achieve your goals and dreams

Visualization is simple; anyone can do it, and we all have the capability to activate it. The best times to do this are in the morning, preferably right after meditation, or before going to bed.

Here's an idea of how to visualize yourself achieving the dream of owning your home:

Find a quiet space where you feel comfortable, sit down, and close your eyes. In as much vivid detail as possible, imagine how your life would be if you were living that dream. Imagine being inside of yourself, looking out through your eyes at the ideal result. Vivid pictures of the home of your dreams, what it looks like, the colors, smell, size, decorations. Imagine you inside your home. What room are you in? What does the room look like? Are your friends and family there? Where in the house are they? Why is everyone there? Feel how happy that it makes you feel to have everything and everyone in your new beautiful home. You're walking toward the yard; open the doors and look out into the sky, see the clouds, smell the air. Now you have activated the power of visualization.

Law of Attraction

Less of the what-if, and more of the now. Tap into satisfying positive thoughts so that you can manifest more of what you want and less of what you don't want. The Law of Attraction is one of the universal laws. It's part of the flow of the universe, so it is definite and happening constantly, just as the other universal laws. Knowing of its existence will give you an advantage toward attracting more of the things you want in your life. Everything, no matter what it is in your life, you have attracted. When you understand that the Law of Attraction is comprised of energy, positive thought patterns, and actions you can attract more happiness in your life. Here's an example of the Law of Attraction taking place:

This Is the Story of Kenya

One of my dearest buyers! She was in the final stages of her homebuying process. She had a cashier's check that got misplaced by a third party. She then went to the bank and was told it would take thirty days to refund her the money. Her closing was in five days, and the seller was not going to allow an extension on her contract. She had no more money to replace those funds to be able to close. The buyer was aware that she may lose her home if she did not have the money to bring to closing. I told her to let the thought go, and for the next few days just to do things that made her happy.

She did not dwell on the problem; she focused on positive thoughts. Instead of going into panic or the blame game (which I will discuss next), she said something that stuck with me: "This home has been anointed, this home is mine. I stood in front of this home and I anointed it the day I saw it, so I don't know how, but it will all work itself out."

She made a declaration that this home was going to be hers and she declared this with true intent. Four days later, she called to say the funds were in her account, just in time. Kenya closed. This is an example of how powerfully your thoughts can align with your wants and the Law of Attraction takes over.

Blame Game

Here is where the mind starts playing games with you. Your realtor calls you and explains there is a situation going on with your transaction and you flip out.

How do you flip out?

Take this buyer I had who was very tight on their monthly payment, so I needed to crunch the numbers. I came up with a solution for how they could reduce the payment by negotiating with the seller to pay for the homeowner association fee for the entire first year.

Finding appreciation in a situation is what makes us better people. This particular buyer was in a mind game riding along with the blame game. I was offering a solution which provided a lower mortgage payment. The next day, the buyer went to the lender's office to discuss this payment option and called me from the meeting. Mind you, I am their realtor not their loan officer. She expressed her concern that the actual payment was thirty dollars off from the approximate payment that we had discussed the night before. I in turn felt very confused about why she would be focusing on a thirty-dollar difference instead of the fact that I saved her $1,200 a year.

Focus on the solution, shift your perspective, and take accountability in order to manifest the outcome you want. Again, we want to focus on that people are helping in the transaction, so we can feel good. The whole point of this chapter is for you to feel good and not blame others for situations and to look at the positive.

The Story of Barbie

A friend of mine was staying on an island. She had been there for many days, but for some reason upon checkout her credit card authorization was fifty-seven cents short. This is not a person who is ever short on money, so she was very upset. She had no access to any other credit cards, no banks in the area, and they did not take cash. She was upset at herself, at the credit card company, the hotel, everyone. Her energy was so off she couldn't even think straight. About an hour went by and still no resolution.

She then said to herself, "I'm going to get it done; I just don't know how." She called a friend for help and her friend said, "Barbie, just ask them to run your card for $4,999.43." Barbie was so focused on the fifty-seven cents that if she would have just changed her perspective, the answer was there the entire time. When you feel things are not going your way, change your perspective and all will manifest. When these behaviors arise, I call this is the **Fifty-Seven Cent Rule**.

Connect with Your Agent

It's important to have a connection with your Real Estate Agent, a sort of chemistry where you feel comfortable enough to reach out whenever necessary. Buyers go through many different emotions during the homebuying process, so a strong support system from your agent has a big impact on your experience. If this is the first time you're buying, this can be an intimidating process. Working with an experienced agent who can coach you through the steps is vital. Once you are under contract, there's much excitement and the thoughts of how life would be different as you see yourself living in your new home start to become real.

Even though you haven't received your keys yet, you begin to feel a sense of ownership. As you go through the process, the threat of losing your home can take a toll on your emotions. You start to think, "What if I don't get approved? What if the home doesn't appraise? What if the inspections don't pass?" All the what-ifs surface, and you start to feel the stress. Your point of contact is your agent, who acts as your confidant and many times your personal therapist. In the story of Michael and Miranda, it was critical to have separated me from her current state of emotion and be able to advise her knowing her life situation. The connection that I develop with my buyers early in the process, knowing their needs, wants, and dreams enables me to guide them to make better decisions for themselves and their family.

Be Happy and Maintain a Positive Attitude

This is a happy time! You are buying your home and it's one of the most unforgettable moments of your life. Focusing on the positive and maintaining a positive attitude is important. Planning your wedding, preparing for college, or buying your first car … all these milestones carried preparation, research, and challenges. How different would these experiences be if your attitude was a negative one? Enjoy the journey and be grateful that you have the possibility to make these dreams come true. Maintain a state of gratitude and allow yourself to have a positive experience. Just as in planning a wedding, the birth of a child, and choosing your college, it's a lot of work to make it perfect, but at the end it's all well worth the effort. As you encounter a challenging moment in the process, decide how you will handle it. Shift your perspective.

Trust in the Process

Trust in the process is really saying, "let go of fear." If you don't allow yourself to trust in the process, you will allow fear to control your choices. Our choices have tremendous power and poor decisions are made out of fear. The choices we make influence our mental, spiritual, emotional, and physical health, as well as influencing the people around us. There is uncertainty in the process of buying a home as it comes with no guarantee. You can choose to experience this dream of buying your home through fear, or you can trust in the process, connect, and your path becomes clear and empowered.

Here are a few tips that if you follow to trust in the process life will work in your favor:

- **Embrace the unknown:** this is exactly where you are supposed to be, and it is a gift to trust the unforeseen with feelings of joy.
- **Live with uncertainty:** let go of your fears, change is coming, and we never know what's going to happen and why things are happening. Believe.

- **Get comfortable with change**: life changes in an instant. Be willing to adjust to these changes, adjust your direction, and refocus to reach your goals.

- **Claim your abundance**: live in a state of gratefulness. Enjoy the gifts you are about to receive. Do not self-sabotage.

- **Go with the flow**: detach from the people, places, and things that do not serve you. Release the negativity.

- **Letting go**: trust your feelings and let go of harmful thoughts.

- **Believe in yourself**: know that you are resilient, believe in your ability to move forward.

The one thing that successful people have in common is that they use visualization techniques to reach their goals. Here's a very simple visualization technique where you can use **Goal Pictures and Affirmations**.

These are physical pictures that you create of your future goals and dreams as if they already realized. If your goal is to own a new home, boat, car, or to travel, take a selfie of yourself in front of the home, boat, or car, or something that is similar. Cut out a picture of your desired travel location. You are creating a dream picture of all aspects of your life including career, family, love, travel, health, and spirituality. Include things you would like to purchase. It can be anything you desire.

Now that you have turned your mental dreams and goals into visual goals, choose an affirmation that puts your dreams and goals into the experience of already having what you want. For example: "I am healthy and happy living in my new four-bedroom home with a pool, traveling to beautiful islands every summer with my family, and driving my new Porsche to my investment banking job." Repeat your affirmation daily as it keeps you focused, motivated, and activates creativity to keep you focused on reaching your goals and dreams no matter what. Repeat the affirmation morning and night, and you will see dramatic results. It becomes part of your automatic thinking and everything you do will lead to making decisions to reach those goals and dreams. This becomes part of your being, and you will not allow anything to come between you and your dream.

Conclusion

THIS IS IT!

This is your chance to make it happen. Stop throwing away money on rent and let go of all those beliefs which limit your ability to move forward in your life to create a stable and safe environment for your family and loved ones. To be able to recognize an opportunity and take it.

I get calls from buyers that have been renting five, ten, and even twenty-five years. If you look at the rent chart in Chapter One, where are you in this chart? There are people who have paid $50,000 to $100,000 in rent payments. Don't stay comfortable. To grow, we have to be willing to reach outside of our comfort zones. Nothing of value comes easy and with effort come great rewards. There's not one buyer that I have worked with who hasn't told me that overcoming their beliefs and fears was worth it in the end. That yes, they entered the unknown, and it was an emotional journey, but if they had to do it all over again, they would. I have had buyers tell me that the homebuying process has been one of the scariest, but most rewarding experiences of their lives.

Working with the Right Team

By now you have read about and are familiar with what to expect in the homebuying process and have some examples of other buyers' stories and the challenges they may have experienced and know how working with the right team can affect your outcome. It's important that when you are faced with any challenges throughout this process you are working with the right team. Just like with sports, it's the collective efforts of every player playing their part to the best of their ability that brings home the win. No one player carries the entire responsibility. Even LeBron James, who is considered to be the world's best player, needs his teammates and coach. Same with buying a home. Your realtor is your coach there to take you to the win.

Allowing Yourself to Be Coached

I have had many buyers that start our meeting by telling me that this will not happen for them. That it's not the right time or they know that they have to wait to buy. They have preconceived notions of why it's not possible instead of focusing on how it can be made possible. These are all limiting beliefs that they have created in their mind. I always take the approach of "What can I do to make it happen?" I explain that there is a way. Whether it can happen today or next month or in the next year, it can be done as long as you are willing to put in the work. Here is an example of a buyer who had no limiting beliefs, trusted in the process, allowed himself to be coached, and made his dream a reality:

The Story of Hans

Hans and his wife, Laura, were a young couple with a daughter who came to me in the search of their first home. Hans had a very challenging situation, as he had a lot of debt and this impacted both his credit score and his DTI. After analyzing his credit report, a detailed plan was set in motion. In order for Hans to make this happen, he would have to pay off a rather large amount of debt, which meant increasing working hours in order not to deplete his savings account and a cram course in managing their money as a family.

It has been said that when you are focusing on a goal life brings you challenges. This is exemplified the saying, "When it rains it pours." Hans worked two jobs and slowly made payments to reduce his debts in addition to his regular bills and rent payment. This meant no holidays, no dinners out, just complete focus on the goal of buying his home. Hans had three monthly car payments. His wife's, a car for his sister-in-law under his name, and his. This was too much for him to qualify with his current income. The sister-in-law had agreed to take over the payments by refinancing the car, as this was his last obstacle.

By this time, he was under contract and going through the loan process. At the last minute, his sister-in-law purchased another car on her own and left Hans with the car payment. Needless to say, this caused family issues and Hans was emotionally devastated after all the work and sacrifice he had put into this. I explained to him that now was not the moment to give up. Hans was not giving up and continued to push forward. He trusted in the process. I asked him to post the car in Swap-a-lease, an online lease trader, and to contact everyone he knew to see if anyone was interested. Finally, somehow, underwriting approved Hans without removing the car. Hans was able to close, and every time I have a buyer who walks into my office saying that it can't happen, Hans is only a phone call away to tell his story and to urge buyers to push forward and allow themselves to be coached. Hans is very grateful, and his words are always, "Please, listen to what she says, it is worth everything I went through to get there."

Connecting with Your Coach

This is the most important connection you need to have throughout this process. This is the person in your corner, the one who represents your best interests and fights on your behalf. This is the person who's going to negotiate for you and protect you if the appraisal comes in low, the seller doesn't want to repair the roof, the lender offers you a high interest rate or your credit needs repair. There are so many pieces to the puzzle to put you in the best light! When you find a coach, who cares and takes pride in their business and isn't looking just to make the next commission check but to establish long-term relationships, that's when you know you are in the right hands.

Obstacles and Their Outcomes

There will always be obstacles to overcome. It's how we handle them that determines our outcome. Hans could have given up many times through his process, and many times he doubted whether or not he would be able to make it through. He allowed himself to be coached, trusted his team, and reached his goal. There will be some unforeseen challenges throughout this process. The important thing is not to panic, but rather focus on a solution. Remember that everyone involved in this transaction has the same goal in mind and that's for you, the buyer, to close on this home. As professionals, we have the experience and expertise to help you navigate through this process and help you reach the most favorable outcome.

Realtor Representation and Coaching

One of the biggest misconceptions that a buyer has is that you will get a better deal and save money if you go directly to the seller or work with the seller's agent. Just like entering into a court of law without an attorney, each party has representation. Why is this? This is because you need someone who's looking out for your best interest. When you do your inspections on the home are you going to want the seller's inspector there or your inspector?

This is the same for representation. In negotiating any terms with the seller, do you want the seller's realtor to fight for your offer or your own agent who makes sure the property you're placing an offer on is appropriately priced so that it will appraise. Will going to a For Sale by Owner or "FSBO" save money? Actually, this only wastes the seller and buyer's time, because FSBO's are typically not properly priced with the market. The sellers have unrealistic expectations about what the property is worth and negotiating directly with a seller only makes you come off as desperate and doesn't allow you to be in a strong negotiating position.

Did you know that Colby Sambrotto, a founder and former chief operating officer of www.forsalebyowner.com, could not sell his home for six months and later sold it with a realtor with multiple offers and full six percent commission for $150,000 more than the original asking price? Not only do you have to deal with all the stress and legalities of the process but now you don't even maximize your selling potential. As a buyer, you don't pay the commission of the realtor the seller does. So, take advantage of the services available to you.

Long-Term Effects

Making the wrong decision at a critical point can be costly and carry long-term effects. Listen to your coach, don't let your fears get in your way. Below are a few examples:

The Story of Charles

Charles went through the entire loan process and when he received his monthly mortgage payment, decided that it was $157 more than what he was willing to pay monthly even though he was approved. Here we go again with the Fifty-Seven Cent Rule! He decided to continue to rent for another year and throw away thousands of dollars every month into a property that is not his rather than invest in a property that was his own for a difference of $157.

This is a perfect example of someone who, instead of shifting his perspective, stayed stuck in the negative and let his fears take over. Not only did he lose his $5,000 deposit on the contract, but he also lost the opportunity to start earning the equity (value) on a property and the $24,000 he paid in rent for the next year. This was a very bad choice. As interest rates rise and home prices rise when Charles attempts to buy again he will have lost well over $157 and thousands of dollars in rent payments. He will also lose the window of opportunity where qualifying and he may be priced out of the market.

The Story of Carly

Carly purchased a home for $296,000. Closing costs were being paid by the seller in the amount of about $12,000. Carly had been renting for most of her life. When the home appraised it came $4,000 under the purchase price. Carly and her family felt the home was not worth paying $4,000 additional and the seller would not reduce the price. Carly made a big mistake. She continued to rent, and a year later that same home was selling for $353,000. I reached out to Carly and sold her a home and she closed. Carly's $4,000 resulted in a loss of $21,600 in rent payments and a loss of equity of about $57,000. A total of $78,600 for not paying a difference in appraisal of $4,000.

What's Next?

You are ready to move forward and work with a strong team to make your homeownership dream come true. You have heard other buyer's stories of how they have been able to make it happen with the proper team and guidance. You understand that you no longer have to rent, there are programs that can help you and you have learned how to create a budget and set goals. You are ready to experience the independence, empowerment and stability that homeownership brings. Together with Homebuyer Rollercoaster and Coaching this can become a reality. Let's start to create your Homebuyer Blueprint today!

ACKNOWLEDGEMENTS

My gratitude is for these important people that have marked my life:

To the most selfless and loving parents and grandparents a daughter can ask for. My father, my example of never giving up. The man who taught me strong work ethics and from whom I inherited my love of gemology, studying, selling, and business. My mother, the strongest woman I know and the woman who has taught me the most important careér of my life, how to be a mother. The unconditional love and support they have given their grandchildren have made my life journey possible.

To my sons, Dante and Dominic, it's that light that you have inside you to persevere, support, and believe in each other, without judgement, that I'm most proud of. Thank you for sharing your light with me by always protecting me, believing in me, and being by my side. This book would not have been possible without you as my inspiration.

The greatest gift Mom and Dad have ever given me is you. So we never have to walk alone on this journey of life. There's no one in the world that knows me better than you. Just like there is no one in the world who will ever love you more than me. My sister Lisa, you have always been there for me, for my children who you love as if they are your own. You encourage me, motivate me, uplift me, and always believe in me. You are the heart and center of all of our lives. Your strength and ability to persevere is admirable. You have the biggest heart of anyone I know and everyone you come close to is blessed to have you in their lives. There have been more than a thousand times I have thanked the stars for you and there will be thousands more.

To my ex-husband and father of our twin sons, Orlando Benitez. Ever since I was a young girl I have admired you, and forty years later nothing has changed. You have my appreciation for the significant amount of love, growth, and support you have given my life. My gratitude will never subside.

For my other sister, Natalie Rey. Life is simply better with you. I will always cherish your unwavering love and friendship, your support in this book, my growth, my family, and my life. Never do you say no, no matter the time or place! For jumping on a plane and meeting me in a moment's notice to help me move my sons into their dorms. For flying out to spend time with my boys even when I'm not there, always looking out for them. I especially love you for your patience when I'm always on my phone. Looking forward to many more memories together. There are still a few islands missing on our bucket list!

To Zenita Barouh, I don't have the words to make you feel what I feel of our love for each other and our families. But I can show you in our hugs. I felt this quote comes close to us: "Friendship isn't about who you've known the longest. It's about who walked into your life and said, 'I'm here for you' and proved it." Love you, Z.

There could have not been a more perfect place to give life to this book than on the island of Islamorada in Florida at La Siesta Resort and Marina. "John's House" is a cottage in a tropical paradise where this book was born. The cottage's gift was not only that it was gorgeous but also the peace you feel while there. Perfect space and décor radiating a sense of calmness and serenity. To add to John's House, as it is named and which I later renamed as "The Authors' Cottage," was the perfect double rainbow that adorned the sky over my stay. Six a.m. yoga in front of a pink sky, breathtaking sunrises, turquoise ocean waters, silky smooth sand beach, and beautiful weather. The wonderful staff that continued to accommodate my stay for more and more days because I didn't want to leave until my manuscript was complete and ready to come into the world with the same feelings the cottage has given me. Thank you for an amazing stay, but most of all an unforgettable memory of where this book was born.

A heartfelt thank you to the special people in my life who have supported me, my crazy work schedule, endless weekends, and late nights.

To all my buyers and sellers that have trusted me and allowed me to coach and guide you and to be a part of such a special milestone in your lives. Allowing me to share your stories in the hopes of helping others and making a difference. Your stories inspired the pages in this book and will serve as a motivation for others to move forward and pursue their dreams. I am grateful every day for the faith you instill in me to have made your dreams come true.

To Dr. Angela Lauria, my book coach and author mentor. Thank you for creating this platform that allows me to reach others and make a difference in their lives through the words on these pages. Even coaches need a coach.

To the Morgan James Publishing team: Special thanks to David Hancock, CEO & Founder for believing in me and my message. To my Author Relations Manager, Margo Toulouse, thanks for making the process seamless and easy. Many more thanks to everyone else, but especially Jim Howard, Bethany Marshall, and Nickcole Watkins.

THANK YOU!

You're thinking of purchasing and you know you want to maximize your experience—that's what led you to this book. This is definitely one of the most important decisions you will be making in your life, and you understand there are complexities to the homebuying process. Now you can achieve faster results with minimum obstacles and the support and guidance needed to have a positive homebuying experience with Homebuyer Rollercoaster and Coaching. If you have learned anything by reading this book, then I feel you are ready to move forward and make your dream come true! Contact me at monica@mpbenitez. com and schedule an appointment to start your coaching and homebuying process and access to my calendar for scheduling. I look forward to being part of such an important milestone in your life!

ABOUT THE AUTHOR

 **Monica Benitez** has been an expert in the real estate industry over twenty years with Residential and Commercial, Construction, Development, Management, and Sales experience. She is also a New Construction, Buyer Coaching specialist guiding buyers in their homebuying process by authentic leadership; managing weaknesses and developing strengths. Finally, she is a Realtor Coaching specialist who helps realtors expand their business. She is an author and Certified Gemologist who resides with her family in South Florida.